TABLE OF CONTENTS

CLASSY WINGS

TANGY BAKED WINGS

MAKES 12 SERVINGS

1   envelope (about 1 ounce) dry onion soup and recipe mix

⅓   cup honey

2   tablespoons spicy-brown mustard

18   chicken wings (about 3 pounds)

1. Stir the soup mix, honey and mustard in a large bowl.

2. Cut off the chicken wing ends and discard. Cut the chicken wings in half at the joint. Add the chicken to the soup mixture and toss to coat. Place the chicken into a large shallow-sided baking pan.

3. Bake at 400°F. for 45 minutes or until the chicken is cooked through, turning over once halfway through cooking time.

BEER-FA-LO WINGS WITH BLUE CHEESE DIP

MAKES 10 TO 12 SERVINGS

Blue Cheese Dip (page 7)

5   pounds chicken wings, tips removed and split at joints

1   tablespoon olive oil

1   cup beer

½   cup hot pepper sauce

1   teaspoon Worcestershire sauce

6   tablespoons unsalted butter

Celery and carrot sticks (optional)

1. Preheat oven to 450°F. Spray large baking sheets with nonstick cooking spray. Prepare Blue Cheese Dip.

2. Combine wings and oil in large bowl; toss to coat. Arrange wings on prepared baking sheets in single layer. Bake 40 to 45 minutes or until crisp and cooked through, rotating baking sheets halfway through baking time.

3. Meanwhile, combine beer, hot pepper sauce and Worcestershire sauce in small saucepan over medium-high heat. Bring to a boil; boil 12 to 14 minutes or until reduced to ½ cup. Remove from heat. Add butter; stir until melted.

4. Remove wings to another large bowl; add beer mixture and toss to coat. Remove to large serving platter. Serve with Blue Cheese Dip, celery and carrot sticks, if desired.

BLUE CHEESE DIP
MAKES ABOUT 2 CUPS

   1 cup sour cream

 ½ cup mayonnaise

 ¾ cup crumbled blue cheese

   1 teaspoon vinegar

 ¼ teaspoon salt

 ⅛ teaspoon black pepper

Combine sour cream, mayonnaise, blue cheese,
vinegar, salt and pepper in small bowl; mix well.
Refrigerate until ready to use.

MAHOGANY WINGS
MAKES 18 SERVINGS

- 6 pounds chicken wings (about 36 wings)
- 1 can (10½ ounces) CAMPBELL'S® Condensed Beef Broth
- 2 bunches green onions, chopped
- 1 cup soy sauce
- 1 cup plum sauce
- 6 cloves garlic, minced
- ½ cup light molasses or honey
- ¼ cup cider vinegar
- 1 tablespoon cornstarch

SLOW COOKER DIRECTIONS

1. Cut off the chicken wing ends and discard. Cut the chicken wings in half at the joint.

2. Stir the broth, onions, soy sauce, plum sauce, garlic, molasses and vinegar in a large nonmetallic bowl. Add the chicken and stir to coat. Cover and refrigerate for 6 hours or overnight.

3. Stir ½ cup of the marinade and the cornstarch in a small bowl. Add the cornstarch and chicken mixture to the cooker.

4. Cover and cook on HIGH for 4 to 5 hours* or until the chicken is cooked through.

Or on LOW for 7 to 8 hours.

SWEET & SPICY CHICKEN WINGS

MAKES 24 APPETIZERS

1   cup PACE® Picante Sauce

¼   cup honey

½   teaspoon ground ginger

12 chicken wings or chicken drummettes

1. Stir the picante sauce, honey and ginger in a small bowl.

2. Cut the chicken wings at the joints into 24 pieces. Discard the tips or save them for another use. Put the wings in a small bowl. Add the picante sauce mixture and toss to coat. Put the wings on a foil-lined shallow baking pan.

3. Bake at 400°F. for 55 minutes or until the wings are glazed and cooked through, turning and brushing often with sauce during the last 30 minutes of cooking.

APRICOT CHICKEN WINGS WITH STRAWBERRY DIPPING SAUCE

MAKES 8 TO 10 SERVINGS

WINGS

- ½ cup POLANER® All Fruit Apricot Spreadable Fruit
- 1 tablespoon vinegar
- 1 to 2 teaspoons hot pepper sauce
- ½ teaspoon chili powder
- ½ large clove garlic, minced
- 2 pounds chicken wings

PREHEAT oven to 350°F. Combine spreadable fruit, vinegar, hot pepper sauce, chili powder and garlic in a medium bowl. Place wings in a large baking dish. Bake 30 minutes; brush wings with sauce during the last 5 minutes of cooking.

SERVE with Strawberry Dipping Sauce.

STRAWBERRY DIPPING SAUCE

MAKES 6 SERVINGS

- ½ cup POLANER® All Fruit Strawberry Spreadable Fruit
- 1 package (3 ounces) cream cheese or reduced-fat cream cheese
- ½ cup sour cream or reduced-fat sour cream
- 1 rounded tablespoon onion soup mix

MIX dip ingredients thoroughly together in a medium bowl.

ORIGINAL BUFFALO CHICKEN WINGS

MAKES 24 TO 30 INDIVIDUAL PIECES

Zesty Blue Cheese Dip (recipe follows)

2½ pounds chicken wings, split and tips discarded

½ cup FRANK'S® REDHOT® Original Cayenne Pepper Sauce (or to taste)

⅓ cup butter or margarine, melted

Celery sticks

1. Prepare Zesty Blue Cheese Dip.

2. Deep fry wings at 400°F 12 minutes or until crisp and no longer pink; drain.

3. Combine *Frank's RedHot* Sauce and butter in large bowl. Add wings to sauce; toss well to coat evenly. Serve with Zesty Blue Cheese Dip and celery.

ZESTY BLUE CHEESE DIP

MAKES ¾ CUP

½ cup blue cheese salad dressing

¼ cup sour cream

2 teaspoons FRANK'S® REDHOT® Original Cayenne Pepper Sauce

Combine all ingredients in medium serving bowl; mix well. Garnish with crumbled blue cheese, if desired.

APPETIZER
CHICKEN WINGS
MAKES 24 SERVINGS

2½ to 3 pounds (12 to 14) chicken wings

1 cup (8 ounces) fat-free French dressing

½ cup KARO® Light or Dark Corn Syrup

1 package (1.4 ounces) French onion soup,
dip and recipe mix

1 tablespoon Worcestershire sauce

Cut tips from wings and discard. Cut wings apart at joints and arrange in 13×9×2-inch baking pan lined with foil.

In medium bowl mix dressing, corn syrup, recipe mix and Worcestershire sauce; pour over wings.

Bake in 350°F oven 1 hour, stirring once, or until wings are tender.

ANGEL WINGS
MAKES 4 SERVINGS

1 can (10¾ ounces) condensed tomato soup,
undiluted

¾ cup water

¼ cup packed brown sugar

2½ tablespoons balsamic vinegar

2 tablespoons chopped shallots

12 chicken wings

SLOW COOKER DIRECTIONS

Combine soup, water, brown sugar, vinegar and shallots in slow cooker; mix well. Add wings; stir to coat with sauce. Cover; cook on LOW 5 to 6 hours or until cooked through.

APPETIZER CHICKEN WINGS

SPICY ALMOND CHICKEN WINGS

MAKES ABOUT 2 DOZEN APPETIZER SERVINGS

- 3 pounds chicken drummettes
- 3 tablespoons vegetable oil
- 2 tablespoons jerk seasoning
- ½ teaspoon salt
- 1 cup slivered almonds, finely chopped

Carrot and celery sticks and pickles (optional)

1. Place drummettes in large bowl. Add oil, jerk seasoning and salt; toss to coat. Cover; refrigerate 20 to 30 minutes.

2. Preheat oven to 400°F. Line large baking sheet with foil. Spray with nonstick cooking spray. Place almonds in shallow bowl. Roll drummettes in almonds until coated. Place on prepared baking sheet.

3. Bake 30 to 35 minutes or until chicken is cooked through. Serve with carrots, celery and pickles, if desired.

OVEN-BAKED SPICY WINGS

MAKES 8 APPETIZER SERVINGS

2   pounds chicken wings

3   tablespoons COUNTRY CROCK® Calcium
    plus Vitamin D, melted

2   tablespoons red wine vinegar

1   to 2 tablespoons cayenne pepper sauce

1. Preheat oven to 450°F. Cut tips off wings (save tips for soup). Cut wings in half at joint. Arrange chicken wings in roasting pan or broiler pan without the rack. Bake 50 minutes or until chicken is thoroughly cooked and crisp.

2. Combine remaining ingredients in large bowl; add cooked chicken and toss to coat. Serve, if desired, with WISH-BONE® Chunky Blue Cheese Dressing.

NOTE: Oven-baking is easier and less messy than frying these classic appetizers.

CRANBERRY-BARBECUE CHICKEN WINGS

MAKES ABOUT 16 APPETIZER SERVINGS

3 pounds (about 27 wings) chicken wings, tips removed and split at joints

Salt and black pepper

1 jar (12 ounces) cranberry-orange relish

½ cup barbecue sauce

2 tablespoons quick-cooking tapioca

1 tablespoon prepared mustard

SLOW COOKER DIRECTIONS

1. Preheat broiler. Place wings on rack in broiler pan; season with salt and pepper.

2. Broil 4 to 5 inches from heat 10 to 12 minutes or until browned, turning once. Remove wings to slow cooker.

3. Combine relish, barbecue sauce, tapioca and mustard in small bowl; stir to blend. Pour over wings. Cover; cook on LOW 4 to 5 hours.

SWEET HOT CHICKEN WINGS

MAKES ABOUT 34 APPETIZER SERVINGS

- 3 pounds chicken wings, tips removed and split at joints
- ¾ cup salsa plus additional for serving
- ⅔ cup honey
- ⅓ cup soy sauce
- ¼ cup Dijon mustard
- 2 tablespoons vegetable oil
- 1 tablespoon grated fresh ginger
- ½ teaspoon grated lemon peel
- ½ teaspoon grated orange peel

    Celery sticks and blue cheese dressing (optional)

1. Place wings in 13×9-inch baking dish. Combine ¾ cup salsa, honey, soy sauce, mustard, oil, ginger, lemon peel and orange peel in medium bowl; stir to blend. Pour over wings. Marinate, covered, in refrigerator 6 hours or overnight.

2. Preheat oven to 400°F. Bake 40 to 45 minutes or until browned. Serve with additional salsa, celery and dressing, if desired.

HONEY-MUSTARD CHICKEN WINGS

MAKES ABOUT 24 WINGS

3 pounds chicken wings, tips removed and split at joints

1 teaspoon salt

1 teaspoon black pepper

½ cup honey

½ cup barbecue sauce

2 tablespoons spicy brown mustard

1 clove garlic, minced

3 to 4 thin lemon slices

SLOW COOKER DIRECTIONS

1. Preheat broiler. Sprinkle wings with salt and pepper; place on broiler rack. Broil 4 to 5 inches from heat about 10 minutes, turning halfway through cooking time. Place in slow cooker.

2. Combine honey, barbecue sauce, mustard and garlic in small bowl; stir to blend. Pour sauce over wings. Top with lemon slices. Cover; cook on LOW 4 to 5 hours.

3. Remove and discard lemon slices. Serve wings with sauce from slow cooker.

ORIENTAL CHICKEN WINGS

MAKES 2 DOZEN

12 chicken wings, tips removed and split at joints

¼ cup plus 2 teaspoons soy sauce, divided

2 tablespoons dry sherry

2 cloves garlic, minced

2 teaspoons packed brown sugar

½ cup mayonnaise

1 teaspoon rice vinegar

½ teaspoon dark sesame oil

1. Combine wings, ¼ cup soy sauce, sherry, garlic and brown sugar in large resealable storage bag. Seal bag; turn to coat. Marinate in refrigerator 4 hours or up to 24 hours.

2. Combine mayonnaise, vinegar, sesame oil and remaining 2 teaspoons soy sauce in small bowl; stir to blend. Cover; refrigerate until ready to serve.

3. Preheat broiler. Drain wings; reserve marinade. Place wings on rack of broiler pan. Brush with half of reserved marinade. Broil 6 inches from heat 10 minutes. Turn wings over; brush with remaining marinade. Broil 10 minutes or until wings are browned and cooked through. Serve wings with mayonnaise mixture.

GARLICKY GILROY CHICKEN WINGS

MAKES ABOUT 6 SERVINGS

1 cup olive oil, plus additional to grease pan

2 heads fresh garlic, separated into cloves and peeled*

1 teaspoon hot pepper sauce

1 cup grated Parmesan cheese

1 cup seasoned dry bread crumbs

1 teaspoon black pepper

2 pounds chicken wings (about 15 wings), tips removed and split at joints

Celery sticks, corn and ranch dressing (optional)

*To peel whole heads of garlic, drop garlic heads into boiling water 5 to 10 seconds. Immediately remove garlic with slotted spoon. Plunge garlic into cold water; drain. Peel away skins.

1. Preheat oven to 375°F. Grease 13×9-inch baking pan.

2. Place garlic, remaining 1 cup oil and hot pepper sauce in food processor or blender; process until smooth. Pour garlic mixture into small bowl. Combine cheese, bread crumbs and black pepper in shallow dish. Dip wings, one at a time, into garlic mixture, then roll in crumb mixture, coating evenly and shaking off excess.

3. Arrange wings in single layer in prepared pan. Drizzle remaining garlic mixture over wings; sprinkle with remaining crumb mixture. Bake 45 to 60 minutes or until wings are cooked through, brown and crisp. Serve with celery, corn and dressing, if desired.

HOT WINGS WITH CREAMY COOL DIPPING SAUCE

MAKES 8 APPETIZER SERVINGS

Creamy Cool Dipping Sauce (recipe follows)

¼ cup chopped onion

2 tablespoons olive oil

2 cloves garlic, minced

1½ cups prepared barbecue sauce

2 to 3 teaspoons hot pepper sauce

4 pounds chicken wings (about 16 to 20 wings)

1. Prepare grill for direct cooking over medium-high heat. Prepare Creamy Cool Dipping Sauce.

2. Combine onion, oil and garlic in medium microwavable bowl. Microwave on HIGH 1½ to 2 minutes or until onion is tender. Add barbecue sauce and hot pepper sauce; stir to blend.

3. Grill wings, covered, 25 minutes or until wings are cooked through. Turn and brush with barbecue sauce mixture during last 5 minutes of cooking time. Serve with Creamy Cool Dipping Sauce.

CREAMY COOL DIPPING SAUCE:
Combine ⅔ cup mayonnaise and ¼ cup ranch-style salad dressing in small bowl. Stir in 3 ounces crumbled feta cheese and 2 teaspoons finely chopped green onion. Cover; refrigerate until serving. Makes about 1¼ cups.

CHICKEN WINGS IN CERVEZA

MAKES 6 SERVINGS

1½ pounds chicken wings, tips removed and split at joints

1 teaspoon salt

1 teaspoon dried thyme

⅛ teaspoon black pepper

1 bottle (12 ounces) Mexican beer

1. Place wings in shallow bowl; sprinkle with salt, thyme and pepper. Pour beer over wings; toss to coat. Cover; refrigerate 2 to 6 hours.

2. Preheat oven to 375°F. Line baking sheet with foil; spray with nonstick cooking spray.

3. Drain wings, reserving marinade. Arrange wings on prepared baking sheet in single layer. Bake 40 minutes or until wings are cooked through and well browned on all sides, turning and basting with reserved marinade occasionally. *Do not brush with marinade during last 5 minutes of baking.* Discard remaining marinade.

GRILLED VIETNAMESE-STYLE CHICKEN WINGS

MAKES 6 TO 8 SERVINGS

3 pounds chicken wings, tips removed and split at joints

⅓ cup honey

¼ to ½ cup sliced lemongrass

¼ cup fish sauce

2 tablespoons chopped garlic

2 tablespoons chopped shallots

2 tablespoons chopped fresh ginger

2 tablespoons lime juice

2 tablespoons canola oil

Chopped fresh cilantro (optional)

Lime wedges (optional)

1. Place wings in large resealable food storage bag. Combine honey, lemongrass, fish sauce, garlic, shallots, ginger, lime juice and oil in food processor or blend; process until smooth. Pour over wings. Seal bag; turn to coat. Marinate in refrigerator 4 hours or overnight.

2. Prepare grill for direct cooking over medium heat. Preheat oven to 350°F.

3. Remove wings from marinade; reserve marinade. Grill wings 10 minutes or until browned, turning and basting occasionally with marinade. Discard any remaining marinade.

4. Arrange wings in single layer on baking sheet. Bake 20 minutes or until cooked through. Garnish with cilantro and serve with lime wedges, if desired.

THAI CHICKEN WINGS

MAKES 8 SERVINGS

- 1 tablespoon peanut oil
- 5 pounds chicken wings, tips removed and split at joints
- ½ cup unsweetened canned coconut milk
- 1 tablespoon sugar
- 1 tablespoon Thai green curry paste
- 1 tablespoon fish sauce
- ¾ cup prepared spicy peanut sauce

  Sliced green onions (optional)

SLOW COOKER DIRECTIONS

1. Heat oil in large skillet over medium-high heat. Add wings in batches; cook 6 minutes or until browned. Remove to slow cooker.

2. Stir in coconut milk, sugar, curry paste and fish sauce. Cover; cook on LOW 6 to 7 hours or on HIGH 3 to 3½ hours or until cooked through. Drain off cooking liquid; toss with peanut sauce before serving. Garnish with green onions.

ISLAND JERK CHICKEN WINGS
MAKES 6 TO 8 SERVINGS

1   cup Hawaiian barbecue sauce

1   can (6 ounces) crushed pineapple, drained

¼   cup packed brown sugar

2   tablespoons lime juice

1   clove garlic, chopped

½   teaspoon grated fresh ginger

   Hot pepper sauce (optional)

2   tablespoons Caribbean jerk seasoning

18 chicken wings, tips removed and split at joints

1. Preheat oven to 350°F.

2. Combine barbecue sauce, pineapple, brown sugar, lime juice, garlic, ginger and hot pepper sauce, if desired, in food processor or blender; process until well blended.

3. Place wings on large baking sheet; rub with jerk seasoning until well coated. Bake 20 minutes. Baste with sauce; discard remaining sauce. Bake 20 minutes or until cooked through.

PICANTE GLAZED CHICKEN WINGS

MAKES 12 SERVINGS

12 chicken wings (about 2 pounds)

1 jar (16 ounces) PACE® Picante Sauce

⅓ cup orange marmalade

2 teaspoons Dijon-style mustard

1 tablespoon sesame seeds, toasted

1. Heat the oven to 425°F. Line a rimmed baking sheet with aluminum foil. Cut off the chicken wing tips and discard. Cut the chicken wings in half at the joint.

2. Heat **1½ cups** picante sauce, marmalade and mustard in a 2-quart saucepan over medium heat to a boil. Reduce the heat to medium-low. Cook for 40 minutes or until the mixture is reduced to ¾ cup, stirring occasionally.

3. Place the chicken into a large bowl. Add the **remaining** picante sauce and toss to coat. Place the chicken onto the baking sheet.

4. Bake for 40 minutes or until the chicken is cooked through, turning the chicken over once halfway through the bake time. Baste the chicken with the picante-mustard mixture during the last 10 minutes of the bake time. Sprinkle with the sesame seeds, if desired.

TIP: You can substitute 24 chicken drumettes (about 2 pounds) for the 12 chicken wings in this recipe.

MOROCCAN SPICED CHICKEN WINGS

MAKES 8 SERVINGS

- ¼ cup orange juice
- 3 tablespoons tomato paste
- 2 teaspoons ground cumin
- 1 teaspoon salt
- 1 teaspoon curry powder
- 1 teaspoon ground turmeric
- ½ teaspoon ground cinnamon
- ½ teaspoon ground ginger
- 1 tablespoon olive oil
- 5 pounds chicken wings, tips removed and split at joints

SLOW COOKER DIRECTIONS

1. Combine orange juice, tomato paste, cumin, salt, curry powder, turmeric, cinnamon and ginger in large bowl.

2. Heat oil in large skillet over medium-high heat. Add wings in batches; cook 6 minutes or until browned. Remove to bowl with sauce; toss to coat.

3. Place wings in 4½-quart slow cooker. Cover; cook on LOW 6 to 7 hours or on HIGH 3 to 3½ hours or until tender.

SPICY KOREAN CHICKEN WINGS

MAKES 6 TO 8 SERVINGS

- 2 tablespoons peanut oil, plus additional for frying
- 2 tablespoons grated fresh ginger
- ½ cup soy sauce
- ¼ cup cider vinegar
- ¼ cup honey
- ¼ cup chili garlic sauce
- 2 tablespoons orange juice
- 1 tablespoon sesame oil
- 18 chicken wings, tips removed and split at joints
- Sesame seeds (optional)

1. Heat 2 tablespoons oil in medium skillet over medium-high heat. Add ginger; cook and stir 2 minutes. Add soy sauce, vinegar, honey, chili garlic sauce, orange juice and sesame oil; cook and stir 2 minutes.

2. Heat 2 inches oil in large heavy saucepan over medium-high heat until oil is 350° to 375°F; adjust heat to maintain temperature.

3. Add wings to oil; cook 8 to 10 minutes or until crispy, browned and cooked through. Remove wings to paper towel-lined plate to drain.

4. Add wings to sauce; toss to coat. Sprinkle with sesame seeds, if desired.

GREEK-STYLE WINGS WITH TZATZIKI SAUCE

MAKES 8 SERVINGS

2 tablespoons olive oil

5 pounds chicken wings, tips removed
   and split at joints

2 teaspoons dried oregano

   Salt and black pepper

2 tablespoons lemon juice

   Tzatziki Sauce (recipe follows)

SLOW COOKER DIRECTIONS

1. Prepare Tzatziki Sauce. Heat oil in large skillet over medium-high heat. Add wings in batches; cook 6 minutes or until browned. Remove to slow cooker.

2. Sprinkle oregano over wings. Cover; cook on HIGH 3 to 3½ hours. Sprinkle with salt, pepper and lemon juice; toss to coat. Serve with Tzatziki Sauce.

TZATZIKI SAUCE: Peel 1 medium cucumber. Slice in half lengthwise. Scoop seeds from both halves of cucumber; discard. Coarsely grate cucumber into medium bowl. Stir in 2 cups plain Greek yogurt, 2 tablespoons lemon juice, 2 tablespoons olive oil and 1 clove crushed garlic. Season with salt. Cover; refrigerate until serving. Makes about 2¼ cups.

THAI-PEANUT GINGER WINGS

MAKES 20 SERVINGS

- 1 can (12 fluid ounces) NESTLÉ® CARNATION® Evaporated Milk
- 1 cup creamy or chunky peanut butter
- ½ cup soy sauce, *divided*
- ¼ cup chopped green onions
- 2½ teaspoons ground ginger
- 2 teaspoons rice or cider vinegar
- ½ teaspoon red pepper flakes
- 5 pounds frozen chicken wings, thawed

PLACE evaporated milk, peanut butter, *3 tablespoons* soy sauce, green onions, ginger, vinegar and pepper flakes in blender; cover. Blend until smooth. Combine *½ cup* peanut sauce, *remaining 5 tablespoons* soy sauce and chicken wings in large bowl; cover. Marinate chicken in refrigerator for 1 hour. Refrigerate remaining peanut sauce.

PREHEAT oven to 425°F. Foil-line and grease 2 baking sheets with sides.

PLACE chicken on prepared baking sheets. Discard any remaining marinade.

BAKE for 40 to 45 minutes, turning once, or until chicken is cooked through. Remove from baking sheets to serving platter. Stir *remaining* peanut sauce and spoon some over wings. If desired, serve remaining sauce with wings and assorted cut-up vegetables.

SERVING SUGGESTION: Jazz up the presentation with a colorful array of fresh vegetables, such as peapods and red and yellow peppers.

TROPICAL CHICKEN WINGS

MAKES 6 TO 8 SERVINGS

1   jar (12 ounces) pineapple preserves

½   cup chopped green onions

½   cup soy sauce

3   tablespoons lime juice

2   tablespoons honey

1   tablespoon minced garlic

2   teaspoons sriracha sauce*

¼   teaspoon ground allspice

3   pounds chicken wings, tips removed and split at joints

1   tablespoon toasted** sesame seeds

*Sriracha is a spicy sauce made from dried chiles that is used as a condiment in several Asian cuisines. It can be found in the ethnic section of major supermarkets, but an equal amount of hot pepper sauce may be substituted.

**To toast sesame seeds, place in small skillet. Shake skillet over medium-low heat about 3 minutes or until seeds begin to pop and turn golden. Remove from heat.

SLOW COOKER DIRECTIONS

1. Combine preserves, green onions, soy sauce, lime juice, honey, garlic, sriracha sauce and allspice in slow cooker; stir well.

2. Add wings; toss to coat. Cover; cook on LOW 3 to 4 hours. Sprinkle with sesame seeds just before serving.

CHICKEN WINGS WITH CHIVE-CAPER MAYONNAISE

MAKES 4 TO 6 SERVINGS

- ⅓ cup mayonnaise
- 1 tablespoon minced fresh chives
- 2 teaspoons capers
- ¼ teaspoon black pepper, divided
- ¼ cup all-purpose flour
- ½ teaspoon paprika, divided
- ¼ teaspoon salt
- 2 eggs
- ½ cup plain dry bread crumbs
- 12 chicken drummettes (about 1¼ pounds)
- 2 tablespoons unsalted butter
- 2 tablespoons vegetable oil

1. For Chive-Caper Mayonnaise, combine mayonnaise, chives and capers in small bowl. Season with ⅛ teaspoon pepper.

2. For chicken, combine flour, ¼ teaspoon paprika, salt and remaining ⅛ teaspoon pepper in large resealable food storage bag. Beat eggs in large shallow bowl. Combine bread crumbs and remaining ¼ teaspoon paprika on large plate.

3. Add chicken to flour mixture; shake well to coat. Dip chicken in eggs, then roll in bread crumbs.

4. Heat butter and oil in large heavy skillet over medium-high heat until butter melts and mixture sizzles. Add chicken in batches; cook 6 to 7 minutes

or until browned on all sides, turning once. Reduce heat to low. Cook 5 minutes, turning occasionally, or until chicken is cooked through. Serve with Chive-Caper Mayonnaise.

JERK WINGS WITH RANCH DIPPING SAUCE

MAKES 6 TO 7 SERVINGS

½ cup mayonnaise

½ cup plain yogurt or sour cream

1½ teaspoons salt, divided

1¼ teaspoons garlic powder, divided

½ teaspoon black pepper, divided

¼ teaspoon onion powder

2 tablespoons orange juice

1 teaspoon *each* sugar, dried thyme and paprika

¼ teaspoon ground nutmeg

¼ teaspoon ground red pepper

2½ pounds chicken wings (about 10 wings), tips removed

1. Preheat oven to 450°F. For dipping sauce, combine mayonnaise, yogurt, ½ teaspoon salt, ¼ teaspoon garlic powder, ¼ teaspoon black pepper and onion powder in small bowl.

2. Combine orange juice, sugar, thyme, paprika, nutmeg, ground red pepper and remaining 1 teaspoon salt, 1 teaspoon garlic powder and ¼ teaspoon black pepper in small bowl.

3. Place wings in large bowl. Drizzle with orange juice mixture; toss to coat.

4. Remove wings to greased broiler pan. Bake 25 to 30 minutes or until juices run clear and skin is crisp. Serve with dipping sauce.

ORIENTAL CHICKEN WINGS

MAKES 32 APPETIZERS

32 chicken wings, tips removed and split at joints

1 cup chopped red onion

1 cup soy sauce

¾ cup packed light brown sugar

¼ cup dry sherry

2 tablespoons chopped fresh ginger

2 cloves garlic, minced

Chopped fresh chives (optional)

SLOW COOKER DIRECTIONS

1. Preheat broiler. Broil wings 5 minutes per side. Remove to slow cooker.

2. Combine red onion, soy sauce, brown sugar, sherry, ginger and garlic in large bowl. Add to slow cooker; stir to blend. Cover; cook on LOW 5 to 6 hours or on HIGH 2 to 3 hours. Sprinkle with chives.

SOY-BRAISED CHICKEN WINGS

MAKES 2 DOZEN

- ¼ cup dry sherry
- ¼ cup soy sauce
- 3 tablespoons sugar
- 2 tablespoons cornstarch
- 2 tablespoons minced garlic, divided
- 2 teaspoons red pepper flakes
- 12 chicken wings (about 2½ pounds), tips removed and split at joints
- 2 tablespoons vegetable oil
- 3 green onions, cut into 1-inch pieces
- ¼ cup chicken broth
- 1 teaspoon sesame oil
- 1 tablespoon sesame seeds, toasted*

To toast sesame seeds, place in small skillet. Shake skillet over medium-low heat about 3 minutes or until seeds begin to pop and turn golden. Remove from heat.

SLOW COOKER DIRECTIONS

1. Combine sherry, soy sauce, sugar, cornstarch, 1 tablespoon garlic and red pepper flakes in large bowl; mix well. Reserve ¼ cup marinade in separate bowl. Stir wings into remaining marinade. Cover; marinate in refrigerator overnight.

2. Drain wings; discard marinade. Heat 1 tablespoon oil in wok or large skillet over high heat 1 minute. Add half of wings; cook 3 to 4 minutes or until wings are browned on all sides, turning occasionally. Remove with slotted spoon to slow cooker. Repeat with remaining vegetable oil and wings.

3. Add remaining 1 tablespoon garlic and green onions to wok; cook and stir 30 seconds. Stir in broth and pour over wings. Cover; cook on HIGH 2 hours or until wings are cooked through.

4. Add sesame oil to reserved marinade; mix well. Pour over wings; sprinkle with sesame seeds.

SWEET AND SOUR CHICKEN WINGS

MAKES 8 SERVINGS

- 5 pounds frozen chicken wings, thawed
- 1 cup REGINA® White Wine Vinegar
- 1 cup sugar
- 1 can (6 ounces) pineapple juice
- ½ cup ketchup
- ¼ cup beer
- 2 teaspoons AC'CENT® Flavor Enhancer
- 1 teaspoon garlic powder
- 1 teaspoon toasted sesame oil
- 1 tablespoon cornstarch
- 2 teaspoons sesame seeds

Bring large pot of water to boil over medium-high heat. Add wings; boil 15 minutes. Use slotted spoon to transfer wings to large bowl.

Combine vinegar, sugar, pineapple juice, ketchup, beer, Ac'cent, garlic powder and oil in medium saucepan; mix well. Bring to a boil over medium-high heat, stirring frequently; cook and stir 4 minutes. Reduce heat to low. Transfer ½ cup sauce to small bowl; stir in cornstarch. Add mixture to saucepan; cook and stir 3 minutes or until thickened. Let cool and thicken further.

Preheat broiler. Pour half of sauce over wings; toss until evenly coated. Place wings on baking pan. Broil 4 inches from heat about 8 minutes per side or until golden brown. Baste with sauce and sprinkle with sesame seeds before serving. Use any leftover sauce for dipping.

BANDITO BUFFALO WINGS

MAKES 6 APPETIZER SERVINGS

1 packet (1.25 ounces) ORTEGA® Taco Seasoning Mix

12 chicken wings (about 1 pound total)

   ORTEGA® Salsa, any variety

PREHEAT oven to 375°F. Lightly grease 13×9-inch baking pan.

PLACE seasoning mix in heavy-duty plastic or paper bag. Add 3 chicken wings; shake well to coat. Place wings in prepared pan. Repeat until all wings have been coated.

BAKE for 35 to 40 minutes or until juices run clear. Serve with salsa for dipping.

GRILLED TANDOORI-STYLE CHICKEN WINGS WITH CUCUMBER-YOGURT SAUCE

Juice of 2 limes

2 tablespoons finely minced garlic

1 tablespoon finely minced fresh ginger

1 teaspoon kosher salt

1 teaspoon chili powder

1 teaspoon garam masala*

3 pounds chicken wings, tips removed

Cucumber-Yogurt Sauce (page 63)

Garam masala is an Indian spice blend that can include black pepper, cinnamon, cloves, coriander, cumin, cardamom and other spices. It can be found in Indian markets and in the spice section of some supermarkets.

1. Combine lime juice, garlic, ginger, salt, chili powder and garam masala in small bowl; stir to make paste. Rub paste evenly over wings; place on large baking sheet. Cover; marinate in refrigerator 2 to 4 hours.

2. Preheat oven to 350°F. Prepare Cucumber-Yogurt Sauce.

3. Bake chicken 35 to 40 minutes or until cooked through. Serve with Cucumber-Yogurt Sauce.

CUCUMBER-YOGURT SAUCE

MAKES ABOUT 1 CUP

1 container (7 ounces) plain Greek yogurt

½ English cucumber, peeled and grated

1½ tablespoons chopped fresh mint

1 tablespoon lemon juice

1 clove garlic, minced

Salt and black pepper

Combine yogurt, cucumber, mint, lemon juice, garlic, salt and pepper in small bowl; stir to blend.

SALSA-STYLE WINGS

MAKES 18 WINGS

1½ pounds chicken wings (18 wings)

2 cups salsa

¼ cup packed brown sugar

1. Preheat oven to 350°F. Line 13×9-inch baking pan with foil. Place wings in even layer on bottom of pan.

2. Stir salsa and brown sugar in medium bowl until well blended; pour over wings.

3. Bake 1 hour or until wings are cooked through, basting every 10 minutes with salsa mixture from pan. Serve with remaining salsa mixture.

JALAPEÑO BLACK BEAN DIP

MAKES 1½ CUPS

- 1 can (16 ounces) black beans, drained and mashed
- 1 cup shredded Monterey Jack or Cheddar cheese (about 4 ounces)
- ⅓ cup HELLMANN'S® or BEST FOODS® Real Mayonnaise
- 1 jalapeño pepper, finely chopped
- ½ teaspoon ground cumin
- ¼ teaspoon garlic powder with parsley

Preheat oven to 375°F. In medium bowl, combine beans, ½ cup cheese, HELLMANN'S® or BEST FOODS® Real Mayonnaise, jalapeño, cumin and garlic powder with parsley.

Spoon into 1-quart casserole, then top with remaining ½ cup cheese. Bake uncovered 20 minutes or until heated through. Serve with your favorite dippers.

HOT ARTICHOKE DIP

MAKES 3 CUPS

- 1   cup mayonnaise
- 1   cup sour cream
- 1   can (14 ounces) artichoke hearts, drained and chopped
- ¼   cup chopped roasted sweet peppers
- ¼   cup grated Parmesan cheese
- 1   can (2.8 ounces) French fried onions (1⅓ cups)

   Assorted PEPPERIDGE FARM® Crackers

1. Heat the oven to 375°F. Stir the mayonnaise, sour cream, artichokes, peppers, cheese and ⅔ **cup** of the onions in a 9-inch pie plate or 1-quart baking dish. Bake for 25 minutes or until hot.

2. Top with the remaining onions. Bake for 5 minutes more or until golden.

3. Serve with the crackers for dipping.

CHEDDAR SALSA DIP

MAKES 2 CUPS

1   can (10¾ ounces) CAMPBELL'S® Condensed
    Cheddar Cheese Soup

¾   cup PACE® Chunky Salsa

2   tablespoons lime juice

    Hot cooked chicken wings

1. Mix the soup, salsa and lime juice in a 1½-quart microwavable casserole. Microwave on HIGH for 2½ minutes or until hot, stirring once.

2. Serve warm with the wings for dipping.

ROASTED RED PEPPER DIP WITH TACO CHIPS

MAKES 2 CUPS

- 2 tablespoons olive oil
- 1 medium onion, chopped
- 3 tablespoons ORTEGA® Fire-Roasted Diced Green Chiles
- 2 teaspoons POLANER® Chopped Garlic
- 2 jars (12 ounces each) roasted red peppers, drained
- ½ cup ORTEGA® Thick & Chunky Salsa
- 2 tablespoons REGINA® Red Wine Vinegar
- 1 tablespoon packed brown sugar
- 1 teaspoon ground cumin
- ½ teaspoon salt
- 1 package (12-count) ORTEGA® Yellow Corn Taco Shells
- Additional salt, to taste

HEAT oil in medium skillet. Add onion, chiles and garlic. Cook until onion begins to brown, about 4 minutes.

PLACE cooked onion mixture into food processor with red peppers, salsa, vinegar, brown sugar, cumin and salt. Process until mixture is puréed. Transfer to bowl and cover tightly. Chill at least 1 hour or up to 48 hours.

PREHEAT oven to 350°F. Place taco shells on baking sheet and bake 10 minutes. Remove from oven and gently break into pieces. Sprinkle with additional salt, if desired. Serve with dip.

MINI MEATBALLS WITH RED PEPPER DIPPING SAUCE

MAKES 8 OR 9 SERVINGS

1 bottled roasted red pepper, drained and coarsely chopped

2 cloves garlic, divided

¼ cup mayonnaise

⅛ teaspoon red pepper flakes (optional)

¼ pound ground beef

¼ pound ground pork

1 cup plain dry bread crumbs, divided

1 shallot, minced

Salt and black pepper

1 egg, beaten

¼ cup vegetable oil

1. For Red Pepper Dipping Sauce, place roasted red pepper and 1 clove garlic in food processor or blender; process until smooth. Remove to small bowl; stir in mayonnaise and red pepper flakes, if desired. Set aside.

2. Mince remaining clove garlic. Combine ground beef, ground pork, ¼ cup bread crumbs, shallot, garlic, salt and black pepper in medium bowl. Add egg; blend well.

3. Spread remaining ¾ cup bread crumbs on large plate. Form meat mixture into 32 to 36 (1-inch) meatballs. Roll meatballs in bread crumbs.

4. Heat oil in large skillet over medium-high heat. Add meatballs in batches; cook 8 minutes, turning frequently until browned on all sides and meatballs

are cooked through (160°F). Drain on paper towels. Serve with Red Pepper Dipping Sauce.

TIP: Some supermarkets sell a meatloaf blend of half beef and half pork; use ½ pound of the blend. Or, if desired, use all pork in this recipe.

NOTE: The dipping sauce may be prepared and refrigerated up to 4 hours in advance. Allow the sauce to return to room temperature before serving.

CHICKEN FINGERS WITH DIJONAISE DIPPING SAUCE

MAKES 4 SERVINGS

DIJONAISE SAUCE

- 3 tablespoons mayonnaise
- 2 tablespoons honey Dijon mustard
- 1 tablespoon lemon juice

CHICKEN FINGERS

- ¾ cup CREAM OF WHEAT® Hot Cereal (Instant, 1-minute, 2½-minute or 10-minute cook time), uncooked
- ¾ cup grated Parmesan cheese
- ¾ teaspoon ground paprika
- ¼ cup milk
- 2 eggs
- 4 boneless skinless chicken breasts (1 pound) Nonstick cooking spray

1. Combine all sauce ingredients in small bowl; set aside until ready to use.

2. Preheat oven to 450°F. Coat baking sheet with nonstick cooking spray. Combine Cream of Wheat, cheese and paprika in shallow bowl; set aside. Combine milk and eggs in second shallow bowl; set aside.

3. Flatten chicken breasts slightly to uniform thickness. Cut into strips. Dip each strip into Cream of Wheat mixture, coating evenly. Dip into egg mixture, coating evenly. Dip into Cream of Wheat mixture again, coating evenly. Place strips on prepared baking

sheet. Lightly coat strips with cooking spray. Bake
6 minutes; turn over strips and bake 6 minutes longer.
Serve with Dijonaise Sauce or your favorite dipping
sauce.

TIP: To create a one-dish dinner, serve chicken
fingers over a crunchy fresh salad.

HOT "CRAB" AND ARTICHOKE DIP

MAKES 6 TO 8 SERVINGS

1   (8-ounce) package cream cheese, softened

½   cup mayonnaise

½   cup shredded Cheddar cheese

¼   cup CREAM OF WHEAT® Hot Cereal
    (Instant, 1-minute, 2½-minute or 10-minute
    cook time), uncooked

1   teaspoon TRAPPEY'S® Red Devil™ Cayenne
    Pepper Sauce

1   teaspoon Worcestershire sauce

1   teaspoon Chesapeake seasoning

1   (9-ounce) jar artichoke hearts, drained,
    coarsely chopped

8   ounces pasteurized surimi (imitation
    crabmeat), coarsely chopped

1   teaspoon ground paprika

    Vegetables, crackers or tortilla chips (optional)

1. Preheat oven to 350°F. Stir cream cheese in medium mixing bowl until softened. Add mayonnaise, Cheddar cheese, Cream of Wheat, pepper sauce, Worcestershire sauce and Chesapeake seasoning; mix well. Fold in artichoke hearts and surimi.

2. Pour into 1-quart casserole dish. Sprinkle on paprika. Bake 30 minutes. Serve warm with vegetables, crackers or tortilla chips, if desired.

VARIATION: For a great snack or appetizer, spread leftover dip on English muffins, and place under the broiler for a few minutes until bubbly and browned. Cut into quarters and serve.

SPICY THAI SATAY DIP

MAKES 1 CUP

- ⅓ cup peanut butter
- ⅓ cup FRENCH'S® Honey Dijon Mustard
- ⅓ cup fat-free chicken broth
- 1 tablespoon chopped peeled fresh ginger
- 1 tablespoon honey
- 1 tablespoon FRANK'S® REDHOT® Cayenne Pepper Sauce
- 1 tablespoon teriyaki sauce
- 1 tablespoon grated orange peel
- 2 cloves garlic, minced

1. Combine all ingredients in large bowl. Cover and refrigerate.

2. Serve with vegetables, chips or grilled meats.

ITALIAN
DIPPING SAUCE
MAKES 8 SERVINGS

1 cup PREGO® Traditional Italian Sauce or Tomato, Basil & Garlic Italian Sauce

2 tablespoons grated Parmesan cheese

Assorted fresh vegetables for dipping

Heat the sauce and cheese in a 1-quart saucepan over medium heat until the mixture is hot and bubbling. Serve with the vegetables.

KITCHEN TIP: This sauce is also delicious served with chicken nuggets, mozzarella sticks or fish sticks for dipping.

SINGLE-SERVE SOUTHWEST DIP CUPS

MAKES 24 SERVINGS

24 foil baking cups (2½-inch)

1 can (about 16 ounces) refried beans

2 jars (11 ounces each) PACE® Chunky Salsa

3 medium avocados, peeled, pitted and chopped (about 1½ cups)

1½ cups shredded Cheddar cheese (about 6 ounces)

1½ cups sour cream

½ cup chopped fresh cilantro leaves

Bite-sized tortilla chips

1. Place the foil cups onto a serving platter.

2. Layer **about 1 tablespoon each** beans, salsa, avocado and cheese into **each** cup. Top **each** with **about 1 tablespoon** sour cream and **about 1 teaspoon** cilantro. Serve with the tortilla chips for dipping.

KITCHEN TIP: Stop traffic jams around the dip bowl! Spoon a few tablespoons of favorite dips into foil baking cups. Guests can cruise by the serving table and pick up a dip cup and some dippers and move on to mingle with other guests.

WARM FRENCH ONION DIP WITH CRUSTY BREAD

MAKES 2 CUPS

1   can (10½ ounces) CAMPBELL'S® Condensed French Onion Soup

1   package (8 ounces) cream cheese, softened

1   cup shredded mozzarella cheese

    Crusty bread cubes or crackers

1. Heat the oven to 375°F. Stir the soup and cream cheese in a medium bowl until it's smooth. Stir in the mozzarella cheese. Spread in a 1½-quart shallow baking dish.

2. Bake for 30 minutes or until the mixture is hot and bubbling.

3. Serve with the bread for dipping.

KITCHEN TIP: To soften the cream cheese, remove from the wrapper and place onto a microwave-safe plate. Microwave on HIGH for 15 seconds.

HELLMANN'S®
EASIEST-EVER
DIPPING SAUCES
MAKES ½ TO ¾ CUP

½ cup HELLMANN'S® or BEST FOODS® Real
or Light Mayonnaise

Stir the following ingredients into ½ cup
HELLMANN'S® or BEST FOODS® Real or Light
Mayonnaise:

For an **ITALIAN DIPPING SAUCE,** stir in 1 jar
(7 ounces) roasted red peppers, drained and finely
chopped, and ½ teaspoon red wine vinegar. Great
for spreading on assorted crackers, thinly sliced
Italian bread or fresh vegetable crudités.

For a **BLUE CHEESE DIPPING SAUCE,** stir in ¼ cup
crumbled blue cheese and 2 tablespoons milk. Great
with spicy chicken wings and barbecued chicken or
beef.

For a **WASABI DIPPING SAUCE,** stir in 3 tablespoons
prepared wasabi and 1 tablespoon milk. Great for
dipping shrimp cocktail or spreading on roast beef or
deli sandwiches for an extra kick!

For a **CREAMY PARMESAN DIPPING SAUCE,** stir in
¼ cup grated Parmesan cheese and 2 tablespoons
milk. Great with fresh celery sticks, bell pepper strips
or bread sticks.

For a **BUFFALO DIPPING SAUCE,** stir in 1 tablespoon
cayenne pepper sauce and 1 tablespoon milk. Adds
great flavor to vegetable crudités.

PARMESAN-CRUSTED FRENCH FRIES WITH ROSEMARY DIPPING SAUCE

MAKES 4 SERVINGS

- 3 medium baking potatoes (8 ounces each)
- 1 tablespoon olive oil
- ⅛ teaspoon salt
- ⅛ teaspoon black pepper
- ¼ cup grated Parmesan cheese
- ½ cup mayonnaise
- 1 teaspoon chopped fresh rosemary *or* ½ teaspoon dried rosemary
- ½ teaspoon grated lemon peel
- 1 clove garlic, crushed

1. Preheat oven to 425°F. Cut each potato into 12 wedges. Toss potatoes with oil, salt and pepper in medium bowl. Place in single layer on baking sheet. Bake 20 minutes; turn. Bake 10 minutes. Push potatoes together on baking sheet. Sprinkle cheese over potatoes. Bake 5 minutes or until cheese is melted and potatoes are tender.

2. Meanwhile, stir mayonnaise, rosemary, lemon peel and garlic in small bowl. Serve as dipping sauce with potatoes.

CREAMY ONION DIP

MAKES 2½ CUPS

1 container (16 ounces) sour cream

½ cup HELLMANN'S® or BEST FOODS® Real Mayonnaise

1 package KNORR® Recipe Classics™ French Onion Soup, Dip and Recipe Mix

Combine all ingredients in medium bowl. Chill, if desired.

Serve with your favorite dippers.

OLIVE TAPENADE DIP

MAKES 4 (¼-CUP) SERVINGS

1½ cups (10-ounce jar) pitted kalamata olives, drained

3 tablespoons olive oil

3 tablespoons FRENCH'S® Spicy Brown Mustard

1 tablespoon minced fresh rosemary leaves *or* 1 teaspoon dried rosemary leaves

1 teaspoon minced garlic

1. Place all ingredients in food processor. Process until puréed.

2. Serve with vegetable crudités or pita chips.

TIP: To pit olives, place in plastic bag. Gently tap with wooden mallet or rolling pin until olives split open. Remove pits.

HEARTY ROAST BEEF SANDWICH WITH PROVOLONE

MAKES 1 SERVING

1 tablespoon HELLMANN'S® or BEST FOODS® Light Mayonnaise

⅛ teaspoon garlic powder

2 slices whole grain bread

3 ounces thinly sliced deli roast beef

1 ounce sliced provolone cheese

1 leaf green or red leaf lettuce

2 slices tomato

Combine HELLMANN'S® or BEST FOODS® Light Mayonnaise with garlic powder in small bowl; spread on 1 bread slice. Top with lettuce, tomato, cheese and roast beef, then remaining bread slice.

TIP: For a great twist, try using ⅛ teaspoon dry wasabi powder instead of garlic powder.

MEATBALL SUB SANDWICHES

MAKES 4 SERVINGS

4 sheets (12×18 inches each) REYNOLDS WRAP® Non-Stick Foil

1 package (16 ounces) frozen Italian-flavored meatballs

1 jar (27¾ ounces) chunky spaghetti sauce

4 sub or hoagie-style rolls

1 cup shredded mozzarella cheese

PREHEAT grill to medium-high or oven to 450°F.

CENTER one-fourth of meatballs on each sheet of REYNOLDS WRAP® Non-Stick Foil with non-stick (dull) side toward food. Top with spaghetti sauce.

BRING up foil sides. Double fold top and ends to seal packet, leaving room for heat circulation inside. Repeat to make four packets.

GRILL 10 to 12 minutes in covered grill **OR BAKE** 15 to 20 minutes on a cookie sheet in oven. Serve meatballs and sauce in sub rolls. Sprinkle with cheese before serving.

REYNOLDS KITCHENS TIP: Heat sub rolls on grill on a sheet of non-stick foil 2 to 3 minutes or until toasted.

PHILLY CHEESESTEAK SANDWICHES

MAKES 4 SANDWICHES

1 box (1 pound 5 ounces) frozen thin beef sandwich steaks

1 tablespoon olive oil

2 large sweet onions, halved and thinly sliced

1 large red bell pepper, cut into ¼-inch strips

¼ teaspoon salt

⅛ teaspoon ground black pepper

1 jar (1 pound) RAGÚ® Cheesy! Double Cheddar Sauce

4 hoagie rolls, split

1. In 12-inch nonstick skillet, cook steaks, 2 at a time, over medium-high heat, stirring occasionally and breaking into pieces, 2 minutes or until done. Remove from skillet; set aside and keep warm. Repeat with remaining steaks. Clean skillet.

2. In same skillet, heat olive oil over medium heat and cook onions and red pepper, stirring occasionally, 15 minutes or until onions are caramelized. Season with salt and pepper.

3. Return steaks to skillet with ½ of the Double Cheddar Sauce. Cook, stirring occasionally, 2 minutes or until heated through.

4. To serve, evenly divide steak mixture on rolls, then drizzle with remaining Double Cheddar Sauce, heated.

BUFFALO CHICKEN SANDWICHES

MAKES 6 SERVINGS

⅓ cup FRANK'S® REDHOT® Buffalo Wings Sauce

4 cups shredded, cooked chicken*

6 large Kaiser rolls, split in half

3 cups shredded Monterey Jack or Swiss cheese

*Purchase a rotisserie chicken.

1. Mix *Frank's RedHot* Buffalo Wings Sauce and chicken in saucepan. Heat until warm.

2. Spoon chicken mixture on bottom half of rolls, dividing evenly. Top *each* portion with *½ cup* cheese. Cover with top of rolls.

3. Heat filled sandwiches in 350°F oven until cheese melts and sandwiches are hot. Cut in half to serve.

HEAVENLY CRANBERRY TURKEY SANDWICHES

MAKES 4 SERVINGS

¼ cup cream cheese

¼ cup cranberry sauce or chutney

2 tablespoons chopped toasted* walnuts

8 slices multigrain or whole wheat bread, lightly toasted

½ pound sliced deli smoked turkey breast

1 cup packed mesclun or spring salad mixed greens *or* 4 red leaf lettuce leaves

To toast walnuts, spread in single layer in heavy-bottomed skillet. Cook and stir over medium heat 1 to 2 minutes or until walnuts are lightly browned.

1. Combine cream cheese and cranberry sauce in small bowl; mix well. Stir in walnuts.

2. Spread mixture on toast slices. Layer turkey and greens on 4 slices; top with remaining 4 slices. Cut diagonally in half.

DINER EGG SALAD SANDWICHES

MAKES 4 SERVINGS

6	eggs
2	tablespoons mayonnaise
1½	tablespoons sweet pickle relish
½	cup finely chopped celery
⅛	to ¼ teaspoon salt
	Black pepper (optional)
8	slices whole grain bread

1. Place eggs in medium saucepan; add enough cold water to cover. Bring to a boil over high heat. Immediately reduce heat to low; simmer 10 minutes. Drain and peel eggs under cold water.

2. Cut eggs in half. Discard 4 yolk halves or reserve for another use. Set aside all 6 egg whites. Place reserved egg yolks in medium bowl. Add mayonnaise and pickle relish. Mash with fork until yolk mixture is well blended and creamy. Chop egg whites; add to yolk mixture with celery and salt. Stir until well blended. Season with pepper, if desired. Spread ½ cup egg salad on each of 4 bread slices; top with remaining bread slices. Slice sandwiches in half, if desired, before serving.

OPEN-FACED STEAK AND BLUE CHEESE SANDWICHES

MAKES 4 SERVINGS

4   boneless beef top loin (strip) or tenderloin steaks, cut ¾ inch thick

Black pepper

1   teaspoon olive oil

Salt

4   slices ciabatta bread

8   crumbled blue cheese

1. Season steaks with pepper. Heat oil in large nonstick skillet over medium heat.

2. Add steaks to skillet; do not crowd. Cook 10 to 12 minutes or until medium-rare (145°F), turning once. Remove to cutting board. Tent with foil; let stand 5 to 10 minutes. Cut steaks into slices. Season with salt.

3. Toast bread; top with blue cheese. Top cheese with steak slices. Serve immediately.

VARIATIONS: Grill steak and thick slices of sweet onion. Separate onions into rings after grilling. Serve steak as directed above and top with grilled onions. You may also substitute wasabi mayonnaise for the blue cheese.

TURKEY & AVOCADO SANDWICHES

MAKES 4 SERVINGS

4   leaves lettuce

8   thin slices deli turkey breast (about 8 ounces)

½   peeled pitted avocado, cut into 8 slices

8   slices PEPPERIDGE FARM® Whole Grain
    15 Grain Bread, toasted

2   tablespoons PACE® Chunky Salsa

1. Divide the lettuce, turkey and avocado among **4** bread slices. Top **each** with **1½ teaspoons** salsa and the remaining bread slices.

MILE-HIGH CHICKEN SANDWICH

MAKES 1 SERVING

- 1 tablespoon HELLMANN'S® or BEST FOODS® Real Mayonnaise
- 1 ciabatta roll, split
- 1 cooked chicken breast (about 3 ounces)
- 1 slice bacon, crisp-cooked
- 2 slices tomato
- 1 ounce sliced Cheddar cheese
- Green leaf lettuce

Spread HELLMANN'S® or BEST FOODS® Real Mayonnaise evenly on roll, then top with chicken, bacon, tomato, cheese and lettuce.

TIP: Toss WISH-BONE® Italian Dressing with an assortment of beans to make a quick side salad.

SMOKED HAM, SWISS & CARAMELIZED ONION SANDWICH

MAKES 1 SERVING

- 1 tablespoon HELLMANN'S® or BEST FOODS® Real Mayonnaise
- 1 seeded multigrain Kaiser roll
- 2 thin slices deli smoked ham (about 2 ounces)
- 2 thin slices Swiss cheese (about 2 ounces)

  Caramelized Onions (recipe follows)
- 2 slices tomato (optional)
- 1 green leaf lettuce leaf

Evenly spread HELLMANN'S® or BEST FOODS® Real Mayonnaise on roll, then top with remaining ingredients.

NOTE: It takes a little time to caramelize the onion, but it's well worth it.

CARAMELIZED ONIONS: Melt 2 tablespoons COUNTRY CROCK® Spread in 10-inch nonstick skillet over medium-high heat and cook 1 thinly sliced medium onion, stirring occasionally, until dark golden brown and very tender, about 10 minutes.

MOZZARELLA MEATBALL SANDWICHES

MAKES 4 SERVINGS

- 1 loaf (11.75 ounces) PEPPERIDGE FARM® Frozen Mozzarella Garlic Cheese Bread
- ½ cup PREGO® Traditional Italian Sauce or Organic Tomato & Basil Italian Sauce
- 12 (½ ounce each) or 6 (1 ounce each) frozen meatballs

1. Heat the oven to 400°F. Remove the bread from the bag. Carefully separate the bread halves with a fork. Place the **2** bread halves, cut-side up, onto a baking sheet.

2. Bake for 10 minutes or until the bread is heated through.

3. Heat the Italian sauce and meatballs in a 2-quart saucepan over low heat. Cook and stir for 20 minutes or until the meatballs are heated through. Spoon the meatball mixture onto the bottom bread half. Top with the top bread half. Cut into quarters.

PROSCIUTTO PROVOLONE SANDWICHES

MAKES 4 SERVINGS

1 loaf French bread

4 teaspoons whole grain Dijon mustard

4 teaspoons cold butter

8 ounces prosciutto or other thinly sliced ham

4 cups spring greens (4 ounces)

2 ounces extra-sharp provolone cheese slices

Cut bread crosswise into four (6-inch) pieces. Slice pieces horizontally almost in half. Spread 1 teaspoon mustard and 1 teaspoon butter on each slice. Divide prosciutto, greens and cheese slices evenly among sandwiches. Wrap each sandwich tightly in plastic wrap. Refrigerate until serving.

NOTE: Sandwiches may be prepared the night before.

AWESOME GRILLED CHEESE SANDWICHES

MAKES 3 SERVINGS

1 package (11.25 ounces) PEPPERIDGE FARM® Garlic Texas Toast

6 slices fontina cheese or mozzarella cheese

6 thin slices deli smoked turkey

3 thin slices prosciutto

1 jar (12 ounces) sliced roasted red pepper, drained

1. Heat a panini or sandwich press according to the manufacturer's directions until hot. (Or, use a cast-iron skillet or ridged grill pan.)

2. Top **3** of the bread slices with **half** of the cheese, turkey, prosciutto, peppers and remaining cheese. Top with the remaining bread slices.

3. Put the sandwiches on the press, closing the lid onto the sandwiches. Cook the sandwiches for 5 minutes (if cooking in a skillet or grill pan, press with a spatula occasionally or weigh down with another cast-iron skillet/foil-covered brick), until lightly browned and the bread is crisp and the cheese melts.

KITCHEN TIP: For a spicier flavor, add a dash of crushed red pepper flakes on the cheese when assembling the sandwiches.

MEDITERRANEAN TUNA SANDWICHES

MAKES 4 SERVINGS

1 can (12 ounces) solid white tuna packed in water, drained

¼ cup finely chopped red onion

¼ cup mayonnaise

3 tablespoons chopped black olives, drained

1 tablespoon plus 1 teaspoon lemon juice

1 tablespoon chopped fresh mint (optional)

1 tablespoon olive oil

¼ teaspoon black pepper

⅛ teaspoon garlic powder (optional)

8 slices whole wheat bread

4 pieces romaine lettuce

4 thin slices tomato

1. Combine tuna, onion, mayonnaise, olives, lemon juice, mint, if desired, oil, pepper and garlic powder, if desired, in large bowl until blended.

2. Top each of 4 slices bread with lettuce leaf and tomato slice. Spoon ⅔ cup tuna mixture over each tomato slice. Top with remaining bread slices. Cut sandwiches in half to serve.

GRILLED CHICKEN SANDWICHES WITH BASIL SPREAD WITH REAL MAYONNAISE

MAKES 4 SERVINGS

- ⅓ cup HELLMANN'S® or BEST FOODS® Real Mayonnaise
- ¼ cup finely chopped fresh basil leaves
- ¼ cup grated Parmesan cheese
- 8 slices whole-grain bread
- 1 pound boneless, skinless chicken breast halves, grilled and sliced
- 8 slices tomato
- 4 slices bacon, crisp-cooked and halved crosswise

Combine HELLMANN'S® or BEST FOODS® Real Mayonnaise, basil and cheese in small bowl. Evenly spread mixture on bread slices. Equally top 4 bread slices with chicken, tomato and bacon, then top with remaining bread.

ITALIAN COMBO SANDWICH

MAKES 1 SERVING

- 1 tablespoon HELLMANN'S® or BEST FOODS® Light Mayonnaise
- 2 slices multigrain bread
- 2 tablespoons chopped marinated artichokes (optional)
- 2 tablespoons sliced hot Italian peppers (optional)
- 2 ounces thinly sliced deli ham
- 1 slice mozzarella or provolone cheese
- ¼ cup baby arugula or spinach leaves

Evenly spread HELLMANN'S® or BEST FOODS® Light Mayonnaise on 1 bread slice, then top with artichokes and Italian peppers. Layer with remaining ingredients, then top with remaining bread slice.

PIZZA NIGHT

GREEK PIZZA

MAKES 12 SERVINGS

2	ready-made whole wheat pizza crusts (5 ounces each)
¼	cup pizza sauce
1	teaspoon oregano
1½	to 2 cups baby spinach, coarsely chopped
2	tomatoes, diced
¼	cup chopped red onion
1	can (2¼ ounces) sliced black olives, drained
1	package (3½ ounces) crumbled feta cheese

1. Preheat oven to 450°F. Place pizza crusts on baking sheet.

2. Spread pizza sauce in thin layer over each crust within ½ inch of edge. Sprinkle with oregano. Arrange spinach, tomatoes, onion and olives over top of pizzas; sprinkle with cheese.

3. Bake 10 minutes or until cheese begins to brown and edges are crisp.

KALE, MUSHROOM AND ONION PIZZA

MAKES 4 SERVINGS

1 package (13.8 ounces) refrigerated pizza dough

1 tablespoon olive oil

1 cup chopped yellow onion

1 package (8 ounces) sliced mushrooms

3 cloves garlic, minced

4 cups packed coarsely chopped kale*

¼ teaspoon red pepper flakes

½ cup pizza sauce

¾ cup (3 ounces) shredded mozzarella cheese

*To trim away tough stems, make a V-shaped cut where the stem joins the leaf. Stack the leaves and chop them into pieces.

1. Preheat oven to 425°F. Spray 15×10-inch jelly-roll pan with nonstick cooking spray. Unroll pizza dough on prepared pan. Press dough evenly into pan and ½ inch up sides. Prick dough all over with fork. Bake 7 to 10 minutes or until lightly browned.

2. Heat oil in large nonstick skillet over medium heat. Add onion; cook and stir 8 minutes or until golden brown. Add mushrooms and garlic; cook and stir 4 minutes. Add kale and red pepper flakes; cover and cook 2 minutes to wilt kale. Uncover; cook and stir 3 to 4 minutes or until vegetables are tender.

3. Spread pizza sauce over crust. Spread kale mixture evenly over sauce; top with cheese. Bake 10 minutes or until crust is golden brown.

CHEESY BLT PIZZA

MAKES 6 SERVINGS

INGREDIENTS

- 1   10 oz. (12-inch) pre-baked pizza crust
- 4   oz. cream cheese, softened
- ¾   tsp. Italian seasoning
- ¼   tsp. freshly ground pepper
- 2   cups shredded leaf lettuce
- 1   cup (4 oz.) SARGENTO® Shredded Colby-Jack Cheese
- ¾   cup chopped fresh tomato
- 7   slices crisp bacon, crumbled
- 1   cup sliced olives (optional)

DIRECTIONS

• Place pizza crust on baking sheet and bake in preheated 400°F oven 5 minutes or until slightly crisp. Remove from oven and cool.

• Stir together cream cheese, Italian seasoning and pepper in small bowl. Spread mixture on pizza crust to within ½ inch of edge of crust. Sprinkle with lettuce, cheese, tomato and bacon. Top with olives, if desired.

HAWAIIAN PIZZA

MAKES 8 SERVINGS

- 1 (12-inch) pizza crust
- 1 tablespoon olive or vegetable oil
- 1 cup (8 ounces) pizza sauce
- ¼ cup (2 ounces) sliced Canadian bacon, cut into quarters
- 1½ cups (6 ounces) shredded mozzarella cheese
- 1 can (8 ounces) DOLE® Pineapple Tidbits, drained or 1½ cups DOLE® Frozen Tropical Gold Pineapple Chunks, partially thawed

BRUSH pizza crust with oil. Spoon sauce over crust. Top with Canadian bacon. Sprinkle with cheese and pineapple tidbits.

BAKE at 450°F. 12 to 15 minutes or until crust is golden brown.

PIZZA MARGHERITA

MAKES 4 SERVINGS

1 cup BERTOLLI® Tomato & Basil Sauce

1 (12-inch) prebaked pizza crust

4 ounces fresh mozzarella cheese, thinly sliced

1 tablespoon BERTOLLI® CLASSICO™ Olive Oil

¼ cup chopped fresh basil leaves

1. Preheat oven to 450°F.

2. Evenly spread BERTOLLI® Tomato & Basil Sauce on pizza crust, then top with cheese. Bake 10 minutes or until cheese is melted.

3. Drizzle with BERTOLLI® CLASSICO™ Olive Oil, sprinkle with basil and serve immediately.

STUFFED SPINACH PIZZA

MAKES 8 SERVNGS

INGREDIENTS

- 1 loaf (1 lb.) frozen white bread dough
- 1½ cups chopped plum tomatoes
- ½ lb. bulk Italian sausage, cooked and well drained (optional)
- 1 tsp. dried basil
- ¼ tsp. dried oregano
- ¼ tsp. pepper
- 2 cups (15 oz.) SARGENTO® Whole Milk Ricotta Cheese
- ½ pkg. (10 oz.) frozen chopped spinach, thawed and squeezed dry
- 1 cup (4 oz.) SARGENTO® Shredded Mozzarella Cheese
- 1 cup (4 oz.) SARGENTO® Artisan Blends® Shredded Parmesan Cheese, divided
- 1 clove garlic, minced
- ¼ tsp. salt
- ½ cup pizza sauce

DIRECTIONS

• Thaw bread dough and let rise according to package directions. Roll two-thirds dough into 11-inch circle on lightly floured surface. Line bottom and sides of greased 9-inch cake pan with dough. Place tomatoes and sausage, if desired, in pan; sprinkle with basil, oregano and pepper.

• Combine Ricotta, spinach, Mozzarella cheese, ¾ cup Parmesan cheese, garlic and salt in small

bowl; spread over tomatoes. Roll remaining dough into 9-inch circle; place over cheese mixture. Pinch edges to seal. Bake in preheated 450°F oven 25 minutes. Spread with pizza sauce; sprinkle with remaining Parmesan cheese. Bake additional 10 minutes. Let stand 10 minutes before serving.

CARAMELIZED ONION CHEESE PIZZA

MAKES 6 SERVINGS

- 1 tablespoon olive oil
- 1 large Spanish onion, thinly sliced
- 2 ounces goat cheese
- 1 (12-inch) prepared pizza crust
- ½ cup (2 ounces) shredded Monterey Jack cheese
- 2 tablespoons MRS. DASH® Tomato Basil Garlic Seasoning Blend
- 2 tablespoons grated Parmesan cheese

Preheat oven to 400°F.

Heat oil in large nonstick skillet. Add onion; cook and stir over low heat 20 minutes or until onion is browned.

Spread goat cheese on pizza crust; top evenly with Monterey Jack cheese. Arrange onions on pizza crust; sprinkle evenly with MRS. DASH® Tomato Basil Garlic Seasoning Blend and Parmesan cheese.

Bake 12 to 15 minutes or until cheese is melted and the crust is crisp.

Remove from oven and cut into 6 wedges.

GREEN GARDEN PIZZA

MAKES 30 SERVINGS

2 packages (8 ounces each) refrigerated crescent roll dough

12 ounces cream cheese

1 cup sour cream

2 tablespoons dry ranch salad dressing mix (about ½ package)

½ of a 1-ounce package dry ranch salad dressing mix (about 2 tablespoons)

¾ cup cucumber slices, cut in half

2 cups broccoli florets

½ cup carrot slices

¾ cup grape tomatoes, cut in half

1. Preheat oven to 375°F. Place dough in single layer in ungreased 15×10×1-inch jelly-roll pan. Press onto bottom and up sides of pan, sealing perforations. Bake 13 to 17 minutes or until brown. Cool on wire rack at least 30 minutes.

2. Beat cream cheese in medium bowl with electric mixer at medium speed until fluffy. Add sour cream and salad dressing mix; beat until blended. Spread over cooled crust.

3. Arrange rows of cucumber slices, broccoli florets, carrot slices and tomato halves on pizza. Cut pizza into 30 rectangles. Serve immediately or cover and refrigerate up to 24 hours.

NIÇOISE PIZZA
MAKES 4 SERVINGS

4 ounces goat cheese

½ cup ricotta cheese

½ cup minced fresh basil

1 teaspoon black pepper

1 (12-inch) prepared pizza crust

2 tablespoons olive oil, divided

1 large red onion, cut in half and sliced

¼ pound fresh green beans, trimmed and
   cut into pieces

1 yellow or red bell pepper, cut into thin strips

3 tablespoons sliced black olives

½ cup freshly grated Parmesan cheese

1. Preheat oven to 450°F. Combine goat cheese, ricotta cheese, basil and black pepper until blended. Spread on bread crust to within ½ inch of edge. Set aside.

2. Heat 1 tablespoon oil in large skillet over medium heat. Add onion; cook and stir 8 to 10 minutes or until onion is very tender and brown. Arrange on top of cheese mixture.

3. Heat remaining 1 tablespoon oil in same skillet over medium heat. Add beans; cook and stir 1 minute. Add bell pepper; cook and stir 1 minute or until crisp-tender. Arrange on top of onion.

4. Top with olives; sprinkle with Parmesan cheese. Bake 8 to 10 minutes or until bread crust is heated through.

CLASSIC PIZZA ITALIANO

MAKES 4 SERVINGS

INGREDIENTS

- ½ lb. bulk Italian sausage (or links with casing removed)
- 1 onion, chopped
- ½ cup diced green pepper (optional)
- 1 cup sliced fresh mushrooms
- 1 (12-inch) prepared pizza crust or Italian bread shell
- ½ cup pizza or marinara sauce
- ¼ tsp. crushed red pepper flakes (optional)
- ¼ cup chopped fresh basil or 1½ tsp. dried basil
- 2 cups (8 oz.) SARGENTO® Shredded Pizzeria Cheese

DIRECTIONS

• Cook sausage, onion and green pepper, if desired, in large nonstick skillet 5 minutes on medium heat. Add mushrooms; cook 5 minutes or until sausage is no longer pink, stirring occasionally. Pour off drippings.

• Place pizza crust on foil-lined baking sheet. Combine pizza sauce and pepper flakes, if desired; spread evenly over crust. Top with sausage mixture; sprinkle with basil and cheese.

• Bake in preheated 425°F oven 12 minutes or until crust is golden and cheese is melted.

QUATTRO FORMAGGIO PIZZA

MAKES 4 SERVINGS

- ½ cup prepared pizza or marinara sauce
- 1 (12-inch) prepared pizza crust
- 4 ounces shaved or thinly sliced provolone cheese
- 2 ounces Asiago or brick cheese, thinly sliced
- 1 cup (4 ounces) shredded smoked or regular mozzarella cheese
- ¼ cup grated Parmesan or Romano cheese

1. Preheat oven to 450°F. Spread pizza sauce evenly over pizza crust; place on baking sheet.

2. Sprinkle with provolone and Asiago cheeses; top with mozzarella and Parmesan cheeses. Bake 14 minutes or until pizza crust is golden brown and cheeses are melted. Cut into wedges; serve immediately.

EASY HOMEMADE PIZZA

MAKES 4 SERVINGS

- 1 (12-inch) prebaked pizza crust
- 1 jar (14 ounces) RAGÚ® Pizza Sauce or ¾ cup RAGÚ® OLD WORLD STYLE® Pasta Sauce
- 1 cup shredded mozzarella cheese (about 4 ounces)

  Pizza Toppings (optional)

Preheat oven to 350°F. Arrange pizza crust on ungreased baking sheet. Spoon on Sauce, then sprinkle with cheese and Pizza Toppings.

Bake 15 minutes or until cheese is melted.

QUATTRO FORMAGGIO PIZZA

BBQ BEEF PIZZA

MAKES 3 TO 4 SERVINGS

½ pound ground beef

¾ cup prepared barbecue sauce

1 medium green bell pepper, seeded
   and sliced into ¼-inch-thick rings

1 (14-inch) prepared pizza crust

3 to 4 onion slices, separated into rings

½ (2¼-ounce) can sliced black olives, drained

1 cup (4 ounces) shredded Colby-Jack cheese

1. Preheat oven to 400°F. Brown beef in large skillet over medium-high heat 6 to 8 minutes, stirring to break up meat. Drain fat. Stir in barbecue sauce.

2. Place pizza crust on baking pan. Spread meat mixture over pizza crust to within ½ inch of edge. Arrange onion slices and pepper rings over meat. Sprinkle with olives and cheese.

3. Bake 8 minutes or until cheese is melted.

TURKEY PIZZAS
MAKES 6 SERVINGS

6 ounces ground turkey

1 package (11 ounces) refrigerated French bread dough

½ cup pasta sauce

1 to 2 teaspoons dried oregano *or* 1 tablespoon chopped fresh oregano

½ cup (2 ounces) shredded mozzarella cheese

17 slices turkey pepperoni, quartered

2 tablespoons grated Parmesan cheese

1. Preheat oven to 350°F. Coat large baking sheet with nonstick cooking spray.

2. Heat medium skillet over medium-high heat. Add turkey; cook and stir 6 to 8 minutes or until cooked through.

3. Unroll dough onto work surface. Cut into six squares. Place squares on prepared baking sheet. Spoon pasta sauce evenly on each square; spread evenly to within ½ inch of edges. Top evenly with turkey, oregano, mozzarella and pepperoni.

4. Bake 17 minutes or until edges are lightly browned. Sprinkle with Parmesan cheese.

SPINACH AND SAUSAGE PIZZA

MAKES 6 SERVINGS

- 3 ounces (1 link) smoked turkey sausage, thinly sliced
- 2 ready-made whole wheat pizza crusts (5 ounces each)
- ½ cup ricotta cheese
- 1 clove garlic, crushed
- ½ teaspoon Italian seasoning
- 2 tablespoons grated Parmesan cheese
- 2 cups baby spinach leaves, coarsely chopped
- 2 plum tomatoes, thinly sliced
- ½ cup (2 ounces) shredded mozzarella cheese

1. Coat large skillet with nonstick cooking spray; heat over medium heat. Add sausage; cook and stir 6 to 8 minutes or until browned.

2. Preheat oven to 450°F. Place pizza crusts on baking sheet.

3. Combine ricotta cheese, garlic, Italian seasoning and Parmesan cheese in small bowl. Spread in thin layer over pizza crusts within ½-inch of edge. Layer sausage evenly over cheese mixture.

4. Sprinkle spinach over sausage. Arrange tomatoes on top and layer with mozzarella cheese. Bake 12 to 15 minutes or until cheese is melted and golden brown and edges are crisp.

STUFFED CRUST PIZZA

MAKES 6 SERVINGS

- 1 package (13.8 ounces) refrigerated pizza crust dough
- 7 mozzarella cheese sticks
- ¾ cup RAGÚ® Old World Style® Pasta Sauce
- 1 small red bell pepper, diced
- 1 cup shredded mozzarella cheese (about 4 ounces)
- 12 slices pepperoni

1. On greased baking sheet, roll pizza dough into 13×10-inch rectangle. Arrange 2 cheese sticks on long edge, then 1½ cheese sticks on shorter edge. Lift pizza dough over cheese sticks and press to seal tightly. Freeze 20 minutes.

2. Meanwhile, preheat oven to 425°. Bake pizza dough 6 minutes. Evenly top with Pasta Sauce, red pepper, shredded cheese and pepperoni.

3. Bake 6 minutes or until cheese is melted and crust is golden.

ACKNOWLEDGMENTS

The publisher would like to thank the companies and organizations listed below for the use of their recipes and photographs in this publication.

ACH Food Companies, Inc.

Campbell Soup Company

Cream of Wheat® Cereal

Dole Food Company, Inc.

Mrs. Dash®, is a registered trademark of B&G Foods, Inc.

Nestlé USA

Ortega®, A Division of B&G Foods, Inc.

Polaner®, A Division of B&G Foods, Inc.

Reckitt Benckiser LLC.

Regina®, is a registered trademark of B&G Foods, Inc.

Recipes courtesy of the Reynolds Kitchens

Sargento® Foods Inc.

Unilever

METRIC CONVERSION CHART

VOLUME MEASUREMENTS (dry)

$\frac{1}{8}$ teaspoon = 0.5 mL
$\frac{1}{4}$ teaspoon = 1 mL
$\frac{1}{2}$ teaspoon = 2 mL
$\frac{3}{4}$ teaspoon = 4 mL
1 teaspoon = 5 mL
1 tablespoon = 15 mL
2 tablespoons = 30 mL
$\frac{1}{4}$ cup = 60 mL
$\frac{1}{3}$ cup = 75 mL
$\frac{1}{2}$ cup = 125 mL
$\frac{2}{3}$ cup = 150 mL
$\frac{3}{4}$ cup = 175 mL
1 cup = 250 mL
2 cups = 1 pint = 500 mL
3 cups = 750 mL
4 cups = 1 quart = 1 L

VOLUME MEASUREMENTS (fluid)

1 fluid ounce (2 tablespoons) = 30 mL
4 fluid ounces ($\frac{1}{2}$ cup) = 125 mL
8 fluid ounces (1 cup) = 250 mL
12 fluid ounces (1$\frac{1}{2}$ cups) = 375 mL
16 fluid ounces (2 cups) = 500 mL

WEIGHTS (mass)

$\frac{1}{2}$ ounce = 15 g
1 ounce = 30 g
3 ounces = 90 g
4 ounces = 120 g
8 ounces = 225 g
10 ounces = 285 g
12 ounces = 360 g
16 ounces = 1 pound = 450 g

DIMENSIONS

$\frac{1}{16}$ inch = 2 mm
$\frac{1}{8}$ inch = 3 mm
$\frac{1}{4}$ inch = 6 mm
$\frac{1}{2}$ inch = 1.5 cm
$\frac{3}{4}$ inch = 2 cm
1 inch = 2.5 cm

OVEN TEMPERATURES

250°F = 120°C
275°F = 140°C
300°F = 150°C
325°F = 160°C
350°F = 180°C
375°F = 190°C
400°F = 200°C
425°F = 220°C
450°F = 230°C

BAKING PAN SIZES

Utensil	Size in Inches/Quarts	Metric Volume	Size in Centimeters
Baking or Cake Pan (square or rectangular)	8 × 8 × 2	2 L	20 × 20 × 5
	9 × 9 × 2	2.5 L	23 × 23 × 5
	12 × 8 × 2	3 L	30 × 20 × 5
	13 × 9 × 2	3.5 L	33 × 23 × 5
Loaf Pan	8 × 4 × 3	1.5 L	20 × 10 × 7
	9 × 5 × 3	2 L	23 × 13 × 7
Round Layer Cake Pan	8 × 1½	1.2 L	20 × 4
	9 × 1½	1.5 L	23 × 4
Pie Plate	8 × 1¼	750 mL	20 × 3
	9 × 1¼	1 L	23 × 3
Baking Dish or Casserole	1 quart	1 L	—
	1½ quart	1.5 L	—
	2 quart	2 L	—

Pictured on the front cover: Oven-Baked Spicy Wings
(page 20).

ISBN: 978-1-4508-9338-1

Library of Congress Control Number: 2014952233

Manufactured in China.

8 7 6 5 4 3 2 1

Microwave Cooking: Microwave ovens vary in wattage. Use the cooking times as guidelines and check for doneness before adding more time.

WINGS AND THINGS

Publications International, Ltd.